PLANNING
INTEGRATED CURRICULUM
THE CALL TO ADVENTURE

SUSAN M. DRAKE

Association for Supervision and Curriculum Development
Alexandria, Virginia

Susan M. Drake is Assistant Professor in the Graduate Studies Department, Faculty of Education, Brock University, St. Catharines, Ontario, L2S 3A1. She has over twenty years of teaching experience in elementary, secondary, and adult education.

Copyright © 1993 by the
Association for Supervision and Curriculum Development
1250 N. Pitt Street, Alexandria, VA 22314-1453
Telephone: (703) 549-9110   FAX: (703) 549-9110

Ronald S. Brandt, *Executive Editor*
Nancy Modrak, *Managing Editor, Books*
Ginger R. Miller, *Associate Editor*
Jennifer L. Beun, *Assistant Editor*
Gary Bloom, *Manager of Design and Production Services*
Stephanie Kenworthy, *Assistant Manager of Design and Production Services*
Valerie Sprague, *Desktop Publisher*

ASCD Stock Number: 611-93025
$8.95

Library of Congress Cataloging-in-Publication Data

Drake, Susan M., 1944–
    Planning integrated curriculum : the call to adventure / Susan M. Drake
    p.   cm.
    Includes bibliographical references (p.   ).
    "ASCD stock number : 611-93025"—T.p. verso.
    ISBN 0-87120-208-5
    1. Curriculum planning.   2. Interdisciplinary approach in education.   I. Title.
LB2806.15.D73   1993
375′.001—dc20   93-9219
                                                                        CIP

Planning Integrated Curriculum: The Call to Adventure

1. Exploring the Process 1

2. The Call to Adventure. 8

3. Leaving the Past Behind 12

4. The Struggle to Change. 19

5. Three Frameworks 33

6. New Beginnings 52

7. Returning to the World 53

8. Hearing the Next Call 54

References. 56

1

Exploring the Process

For the past three years I have been deeply involved in the process of creating integrated curriculum as a developer, implementor, workshop leader, and researcher. Talking to people involved in similar endeavors, I invariably met rolled eyes, groans, and epithets such as "a nightmare," "impossible," or "a battle." The consensus seemed clear: developing integrated curriculum collaboratively was a challenge in the best sense of the word. But as I followed different teams at different points in the process, I was fascinated to discover that the "impossible nightmares" faded and were replaced by much more positive interpretations once a writing team actually began to implement integrated curriculum. The team could then go on to plan the next units with some degree of ease, and everyone could begin to talk about how rewarding the experience had been.

These teams seemed to have forgotten most of their initial struggles. Their stories matched my own experiences so well, I began to wonder whether there were universal aspects that most people might expect to experience when undertaking such an endeavor. By listening to others, could I identify commonalities that would lead to a clearer understanding of the problems involved in planning integrated curriculum? These questions intrigued me and led me to further explore the process of developing integrated curriculum.

Making Sense of Curriculum Integration

Is there really a need to develop integrated curriculum, or is it just another passing fad? This question deserves to be examined carefully. We live in a global society characterized by ever-accelerating change, technological advances, a knowledge explosion, changing economic and social realities, and, perhaps, impending environmental disaster. The educational system seems to be constantly under attack. Critics claim that students are dropping out at an alarming rate. Those who stay in school are not doing well enough to be able to compete in a global economy and maintain a high standard of living.

In many districts there has been a demand for a restructuring in education to shift it to decentralization and site-based management. Teachers have been empowered as decision makers; this includes curriculum development. This shift has often led teachers to integrate the traditional subject areas because it made sense to those educators at the grassroots level.

It is important to understand the context of integration as an idea with an intellectual history. Disciplines were artificially created by humans to organize their world, and were often defined by political needs (Beane 1991). Eisner (1992) points out that as early as the 1920s the progressive movement in education advocated curricular integration through themes because proponents believed the disciplines prevented students from seeing the relationships between subjects and therefore decreased the content's relevance. In the '60s, based on Jerome Bruner's (1960) concept of curriculum development, there was a shift to discipline-oriented curriculums where the structure of the discipline was considered to be the facilitator for the storage and retrieval of knowledge. Still, many students today move from science to history to math classes and are taught in a fragmented, disconnected way that has little resemblance to real life.

Today, some people criticize educators for not adequately teaching basic skills; others argue that the basic skills students will need for the 21st century are not the same skills that we are now teaching. The knowledge component of virtually every subject area is proliferating at an ever-increasing rate. Paradoxically, as distinct subject areas become overloaded, a surprising amount of duplication is occurring across classrooms. Educators are caught in a dilemma. Integration, by reducing duplication of both skills and content, begins to allows us to teach more. It also gives us a new perspective on what constitutes basic skills.

The concept of integrated curriculum makes sense for other reasons. Students who drop out perceive little relevance in school life. Integration connects subject areas in ways that reflect the real world. When we set curriculum in the context of human experience, it begins to assume a new relevance. Higher-order thinking skills become a necessity as students begin to grapple with real issues and problems that transcend the boundaries of disciplines. Current newspapers offer an abundance of real-life issues that could be explored from a problem-based perspective. Conscious of age-appropriateness and student interest, the teacher may design problem scenarios based on reality; for example, issues that pit jobs versus the environment, the influence of media in shaping reality, violence in our society, schools and sports, the ethics of genetic engineering, or social issues such as AIDS, poverty, or the war on drugs. Current problems in these areas can be explored from a content perspective, but in searching for practical solutions they also require higher-order thinking skills that transcend both the content and the procedures of disciplines.

Another important consideration is how people learn. Recent brain research indicates that the brain searches for patterns and interconnections as its way of making meaning (Caine and Caine 1991). If humans do learn by connection-making, it only makes sense to teach through connections.

First Efforts

A rationale for curriculum integration seems clear; however, there are few models available to guide us in developing such curriculum. Those beginning the process often feel as if they are in uncharted territory. The purpose of this booklet is to explore some of the territory ahead.

This exploration involves a synthesis of the experiences of several different school districts in Ontario. However, through dialogue and working with others throughout North America, I have come to believe that the process of developing integrated curriculum is universal in many respects. The common experiences identified here will hopefully extend beyond Ontario to offer a helpful guide for others.

In response to some of the criticisms of today's educational system, Ontario chose to focus on increasing relevance in the "transition years" (grades 7 to 9) as explored in such documents as Hargreaves and Earl's (1990) *Rights of Passage*. Uncertain of how to go about this task, the government set up a consultation process. This process involved a committee headed by Gerry Connelly that traveled across the province to consult with community teachers, principals, students, and parents in an effort to rethink traditional models and values. The government funded 66 grass roots projects. The committee followed the progress of these projects during the consultation process.

As a part of this initiative, the government announced an intent to provide a common curriculum for all learners. This involved eliminating the time allocations in terms of being defined by subjects and the designation of programs such as basic, general, and advanced in grade 9. In response to the challenge to eliminate streaming (tracking) difficulties in grade 9 and in an effort to increase meaning and relevance, many schools focused on integrating the curriculum. They did this in a wide variety of ways limited only by the imaginations of the curriculum developers and the support of their schools and districts. At the same time, many schools that did not receive funding for transition years projects were inspired to explore innovative ways to answer some of their educational dilemmas.

Given the freedom to innovate, many schools came up with creative solutions. The results of these explorations during the transition years initiative are guiding the educational policy currently being developed at grades 1 to 9. The major thrust of this policy is to educate the citizens of the 21st century. The emphasis is on clear expectations (knowledge, skill, and values) for students to attain by the end of their primary, junior, and transition years. These expectations reflect an integrated, holistic approach to curriculum. This policy is expected to be extended until graduation.

Integration was a conscious effort to connect curriculum areas that had not previously been connected. I was astonished by the vast differences in interpretation of what integration might be and how it might work. These differences become clear in the following list of some Ontario explorations that range from grades 6 to 12 and involve gifted, learning disabled, and mixed ability groupings:

• Subdisciplines such as auto mechanics, graphics, welding, electricity, and woodworking were integrated into a broad-based technology approach at the provincial level.

• Integrated curriculum was written at central office for the early childhood years.

• A theme or issue was being infused into existing curriculums. For example, the International Joint Commission of the Great Lakes worked on infusing environmental issues into existing science and social studies courses.

• One teacher working on an existing course of study adapted it in a way that connects to other subjects.

• A group of teachers from one school developed curriculum together, but each teaches independently in a separate classroom.

• Another group of teachers developed, team taught, and evaluated curriculum together.

• Use of "curriculum merges" or "curriculum links" integrated various subject areas. This has been done in a variety of ways. In one high school, grade 9 classes met during the first period of the day. At other schools, teachers who see subject connections chose to work together.

• Some newly built schools have had the luxury of a principal who began with a new vision and new staffs to match that vision. In these instances, the schools have been able to move more quickly than others toward integration across the curriculum. There are several examples of this phenomenon, ranging from K-8 schools to a school that initially included only grades 9 and 10 but eventually moved to include 11 and 12.

• One high school has organized all curriculums around the environment. Another high school is organizing around technology as an integrating focus.

Gathering the data for this exploration involved various strategies. On some occasions, I interviewed several key players on an integration team. At other times, I was involved in inservicing with a district. I also attended planning meetings and presentations on curriculum integration whenever possible. I led a provincial curriculum team that developed a K-12 transdisciplinary curriculum based on story as the organizing principle (Drake et al. 1992). During this experience I kept a journal that I shared with my colleagues; this facilitated a mutual understanding of the process.

During this exploration I interacted with many people who were involved in integrated projects from several different districts. I am deeply grateful to those who so generously gave their time to share their experiences with me. I have chosen to name only a handful of these people in this account; however, the experiences of the many others are reflected in the stories that are offered.

I found that the process does get easier. One Ontario district, deeply involved in integrating at a systemwide level, reports that new teams beginning the journey are "light years ahead" of the groups that originally embarked into the uncharted territory. These newer groups have the advantage of reading materials such as Jacobs' (1989) *Interdisciplinary Curriculum: Design and Implementation*, Tchudi's (1991) *Travels Across The Curriculum: Models for Interdisciplinary Learning*, and the *Educational Leadership* (October 1991) issue on integration. They are also able to talk to those who are currently implementing their integration ideas. Collectively they are beginning to identify the process that leads to success.

Nevertheless, the process outlined here may sound pessimistic. The descriptions are not intended to be frightening, but realistic. In asking several of the people represented on these pages if I should soften the experience, the response was uniform. For them, *undergoing the process was the most important aspect of developing integrated curriculum*; they believed it is essential to know that there is indeed a struggle ahead. It is just as important to know that the journey is worth taking and that the process gets easier once you have been through it.

This interpretation is not offered as a "truth," for much of the process is still taking place in uncharted territory. It is offered in the hopes that it may increase understanding for others who are undertaking ventures like ours.

The Journey Metaphor

When I began the project with my own curriculum team, I offered the metaphor of a journey as a guide for the process ahead. This journey was based on my interpretation of the "Journey of the Hero" developed for an earlier integrated studies project (Miller et al. 1990); later, I applied this metaphor to organizational change (Drake 1990) and to individuals involved in significant new learning (Drake 1991). Since this venture involved both experiencing organizational change and significant new learnings, the model seemed to fit.

This journey metaphor worked well for us, a team of six strangers who were well aware of the obstacles ahead. We could have spent all the allotted time dwelling on our perception that there was not a school system in Ontario that offered a realistic structure in which to teach such a curriculum. (In two years this has shifted dramatically.) The metaphor allowed my team to move past the impossibility of the project into navigating new territory with a positive risk-taking attitude.

Listening to others, I was struck at how often I heard the metaphor of "journey." For one district the process was a journey of continually extending their boundaries and learning more. For a high school it was a "voyage of discovery" that primarily involved process rather than product. Karen Erskine, a principal of a K-8 school, comforted her integrated team during times of stress with the metaphor of a ship sailing through choppy waters to get to a safe shore. Fullan and Miles (1992) also use the metaphor of journey for educational change, acknowledging that it is a process of moving through largely uncharted territory.

The "Journey of The Hero" is the basis for most of our stories throughout time and across cultures. According to noted mythologist Joseph Campbell (1988), this quest can be interpreted metaphorically as a blueprint for successful transition. The hero is called to adventure; he or she leaves the kingdom in search of this adventure. Ahead are the demons to be confronted, the dragons to slay. Often the hero is aided by a magic helper such as a magic sword. Finally, the hero slays the dragon, receives a reward, and returns to the kingdom where he or she must share the lessons of the journey.

For educators, the journey could be interpreted as five stages in developing integrated curriculum (Figure 1.1). The heroes as curriculum writers hear a *call to adventure* and enter the world of integrated curriculum.

They leave behind traditional methods of curriculum development and experience *endings* accompanied by loss. This is followed by a *struggle* as they encounter anxiety, conflict, and the excitement of stepping into the unknown. Finally they reach the *reward* and personal satisfaction of truly understanding how to integrate curriculum. The last stage is *service* where the heroes, feeling fulfilled, share what they have learned with other interested educators.

FIGURE 1.1
THE JOURNEY

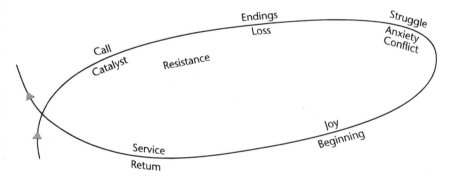

Figure 1.1 illustrates the journey as a spiral to indicate a sense of coiling, ever-evolving growth. The graphic is somewhat misleading because it is too pat. It is only in looking back that it is possible to get the sense of a linear path that has a definite pattern. *Although these stages may seem to be presented as linear, they are most often experienced as chaotic and as "two steps forward and one step back."* I have found that individuals understand the journey by reflecting on how it matches any major transition they have undergone in their own lives. Understanding a predictable pattern of change is helpful in planning how to navigate the journey ahead.

2

The Call to Adventure

Educators are being called to adventure. The catalyst may be either their critics or a sense that there are more relevant ways of educating students. Integration offers an exciting challenge. There are several things to consider at this stage concerning the phenomenon of resistance and the exigencies of planning.

Resistance

A natural human reaction to impending change is resistance. More than one team leader reported that a typical beginning has been to say "It can't be done." Fullan and Miles (1992) caution that we shouldn't even use the word resistance. This initial reaction would be better understood as coming to personal meaning. Rather than bemoaning resistance, we need to support people through this first reaction.

Teachers will offer some solid reasons for resistance such as:
- "This is just a fad; ignore it long enough and it will go away."
- "I'm not interested in change for change's sake."
- "I'm not fixing what already works."
- "I am already integrating in my subject area."

As we move into a world in which knowledge is proliferating at a fantastic rate, it is hard to conceive of integration as a fad. We simply can't keep adding to the curriculum. As I heard over and over "we need to add by subtracting."

Most teachers are already doing a good job. I found that educators resisted the need to integrate when they felt that a personal attack was being made on their current teaching. Claire Ross, principal of Holy Family Education Center, offers a helpful perspective: "It's not that we haven't been doing a good job—we have, but the world is changing and we must change with it."

True, many teachers are currently integrating in their own areas. Yet, from a global perspective a more inclusive view of integration may be more appropriate.

Planning

Setting out on the journey, it is best to plan for the knowns with a collaborative vision of the destination. The vision is often very hazy and "when you get there, it's never how you thought it would be." However, to borrow K-8 principal Karen Erskine's metaphor, "without some description of the safe haven the ship is sailing toward, it will no doubt be destined to forever cruise the choppy waters or return to the familiar shores it left behind."

Some aspects that need to be explored are philosophical: *What is worth knowing? What is the image of the learner? How do students learn?* and *What values are important?* With a vision in place, it is possible to address some of the more obvious questions. The following is a synthesis of answers recommended by a variety of groups.

Who Should Be Involved?

Many teams start with numbers as large as 13; this may include all teachers in one school or include others such as central office consultants. This is clearly an attempt to involve everyone, but most conclude it is too many; they tend to break into smaller groups anyway. My team worked well with six individuals from different subject areas; others report good success with four people. One experienced team leader found an even number seemed to work better than an odd number. Given group dynamics, it seems that any number over seven is too many for constructive work to emerge.

Initial efforts in a district often include representatives from different schools writing together; the expectation is that each representative will act as a messenger and take the process back to others in their own school. In practice, this hasn't worked as well as expected; the writers also need to be able to implement collaboratively. This creates a greater sense of ownership and a greater understanding of the process itself. As teams work together they get good at the process and curriculum planning becomes infinitely easier.

Only those who volunteer should be involved. Usually there are a few enthusiastic participants, some who are there "in case something good might happen," and those who are "brick walls." Reflecting on sometimes painful experiences, many team leaders recommended letting the "brick walls" go. It may seem like this person's subject area is necessary and there will be an important gap in the curriculum design. However, a brick wall, regardless of subject area, can sabotage the whole project. Accept the limitations and begin with people who are willing to innovate and take risks.

According to the experiences of many, the members of an ideal writing team:

- Are volunteers
- Will implement the product
- Love teaching and students
- Are willing to learn
- Are risk-takers
- Demonstrate interpersonal skills
- Perceive the teacher as a facilitator
- Are generalists who "love" a specialized area or
- Are specialists interested in a generalized approach
- Are innovative and creative
- Have taught several subjects
- Are technologically literate

What Form Should Integration Take?

Integration can occur in many different forms and combinations. Perceptions of top-down mandates of how to integrate have often been met with almost reflex-like resistance. Allowing groups to come to their own sense of meaning of "what," guided by a collaborative vision is important. Others, seeing the energy and enthusiasm of those actively involved, are often inspired to join. "Show them that their jobs will be easier" or "better" has convinced many who are hesitant to make a true commitment.

How Much Time Do We Need and Where Should We Work?

The amount of time people spent planning varied from five days, to a month, to a year. Planning seemed to work best when teachers were allowed blocks of time. One or two full days of orientation sets integration in a positive and supportive context. Orientation sessions in which outside "experts" offered a vision of integrated curriculum and some practical strategies were helpful. Subsequent sessions seemed to be most effective when teams were allocated half a day.

Planning time seemed to be most successful when it occurred outside of a school setting. This was particularly true for the initial sessions. My team, funded by the Ontario Curriculum Superintendents' Cooperative, had the luxury of meeting at a hotel in a central location. Other projects have met at a district retreat setting; one team did its best writing over two weeks in the summer at one member's house. Talking over food and drink in the relaxed forum of an outside setting increased feelings of collegiality.

How Do We Do It?

In the final analysis, integration takes "jumping in and doing it." The jumping in can take many forms. Some teams spend a year in preparation. Others are less cautious. One participant commented: "Everyone else has dipped their toes in the water. We jumped in head first. That's how my father taught me to swim."

Successful teams evolved "comfort zones of integration." One integration team consisting of Peter Marshall, Sally Friedenberg, Raquel Ahearn, and Jerry DuQuetteville collaborated for two years through grades 6 and 7. They described this comfort zone as a "balance between working together and respecting that each member will interpret things differently in the classroom . . . and that's okay." The process seems best as an ongoing process of both planning and implementation. Together, through collaboration and personal experience, the team members come to develop this "comfort zone," however, not without having to navigate the path of the journey ahead.

3

Leaving the Past Behind

When integrating curriculum, many things will stay the same. However, the paradox is that the beginning of the journey involves endings. Endings are painful. Accompanying anticipation is a sense of loss and anxiety. Humans resist the journey into the new by clinging to the old, even when it doesn't work anymore. When implementing innovations, educators often tend to add even more to what already exists rather than stop certain practices. Because this just increases the workload, good intentions may be dropped and schools return to their old habits. Therefore, it is helpful to be as explicit as possible about what must end as well as what will continue as before. We also need to be aware of how people experience loss, and acknowledge and support these feelings.

Some endings will be obvious. However, more difficult are the endings that are not conscious. For example, when building integrated curriculum, we must let go of our old models of curriculum design. This is particularly difficult because our old models and accompanying beliefs are often implicit. To further complicate the issue, everyone seems to bring diverse models and beliefs to the writing table.

One thing quickly becomes clear: the old models won't work for this process. Individuals need to become conscious of their current models and beliefs; it seems that only by making beliefs explicit can people move on to discover new ways of doing things.

Letting Go of Old Beliefs

These are a few of the typical assumptions that have shifted as curriculum developers have become more deeply involved:

The Students Won't Learn Basic Skills. Integration does not negate the basic skills. The teachers know what students need to learn. For example, literacy and numeracy can, and should, be built into the curriculum as it is applied in its situational context.

Optimum Learning Moves From Basics to More Complex Structures. Moving from the basic to the more complex has been called the "layer cake" curriculum in which, for example, students move from addition and subtraction to calculus, from grammar to literature, from the periodic tables to chemical equations. Tchudi (1991) argues that it is much better to present students with the big picture: to be able to see the disciplines in the context of real-life problems.

Content is Most Important. Curriculum designers quickly discovered that content, while important, was not the most important element. This is not to suggest that students will not be learning content but that content becomes a vehicle for essential learnings.

Course Content Will Not Be Covered. In fact, many teachers have found that course content can be more effectively covered through integration. This usually involves integrating existing course content such as history and English (rather than letting a theme guide the process). From this perspective, a more selective targeting of the prescribed content makes it more relevant. This approach is helpful for those locked into state or provincial requirements. When subject areas were integrated with others, subject-specific curriculum guidelines constructed for the discipline were no longer as useful. Content that emerges through themes can lead to different course content. Here, the knowledge component becomes a vehicle for achieving essential learnings. For example, a French teacher was concerned that she couldn't teach the sequential skills in her mandatory 40-minute day class. However, when she let go of her belief in the necessity to sequence skills, she found ample places to make French meaningful to the theme. Students seemed to enjoy her classes more and really were learning French even though she couldn't claim to be on page 14 of the textbook.

Integrated Curriculum Is Superficial. Unfortunately, some of the first attempts at integration resulted in superficial products. However, integration can and does lead to curriculum that explores topics in depth and is meaningful and relevant.

Knowledge Belongs in Discrete Categories. Teachers trained in a specialization tend to believe this is true. However, usually when they are able to experience first-hand how their area connects to other areas, they quickly discover that disciplines are indeed structures that humans have devised to organize experience. At this time most educators agree that the disciplines won't entirely disappear; specialists are needed to advance knowledge in specific areas, but perhaps within the context of a generalist perspective. Many contend students need to see a bigger picture and recommend specialization be delayed as long as possible.

Math (or Any Subject) is a "Force-Fit." Math is one area often perceived as a force-fit. For example, one district had a totally integrated curriculum except for a separate math class. The math specialist could see ways math could fit nicely into the existing integrated program, but she was tied to the district's standardized testing process. The force-fit then was mandated by the district requirements, not by the concept of integration.

The subject perceived as a force-fit is often the subject area not properly represented on a team. My own writing team could not fit music in our document; the music specialist easily found a place. This type of experience was told to me over and over again and reinforces the need for representation of as many subjects as possible.

Teachers Don't Know Enough. In fact, teachers know a lot more than they sometimes acknowledge. However, they have to let go of the need to be in control, to know everything. They need to be confident enough to be a learner; to tell students, "I'm not quite sure, let's find out together." One district frames this as a tremendous opportunity for the teacher, as a life-long learner, to learn more.

Integration Is Only for Gifted Students. A common myth is that only the gifted student can make connections. Educators I talked to were developing integrated curriculum for learners of all types. More than one project focused on the at-risk student; they claimed that this type of student benefitted most from the integrated approach because the increased relevance meant increased motivation. In Ontario, integration emerged at the grass roots level as a solution to streaming problems.

The Student Is a Passive Learner. Most educators perceived the student to be an active learner who constructed meaning. The teacher, as facilitator, helped the student with the construction of this meaning in an interactive process. However, in most projects the teacher was in charge of curriculum design; the teacher chose the theme and created meaningful learning experiences.

As teams became more experienced and learned that students can and do ask valuable questions, there was a shift to the curriculum being more student-driven. Students, rather than the teacher, created their own connecting webs to access the known and to develop relevant and pertinent questions. Students answered their own questions and presented them to the class in creative, interesting ways. This teaching strategy takes curriculum control out of the teacher's hands and places it firmly in the student's. In Tchudi's words, "When given an honest chance to explore and shown that their ideas are valued, any group of youngsters from kindergarten and up will raise significant and valuable issues" (1991, p. 38).

Initiating the Endings

Most teams begin to invite endings with some sort of formal orientation. One or two full-day sessions seem most fruitful. Some of the ways in which this orientation has been approached follow.

Integration As an Authentic Path

It is important for teachers to reflect on the necessity for educational change. If integration isn't an authentic path with improved learning outcomes, the resistors may be right; this is just another fad. Campbell (1988) in his journey interpretation suggests that the path must be a "path with heart"; that is, the journey should only be undertaken when individuals believe it is an authentic path for students. Although this may seem like a corny expression, people tend to resonate with the concept of the path with heart. Committing to such a path doesn't make the struggle easier, but it does give a sense of meaning and purpose to the journey.

I usually begin orientation sessions with the journey metaphor and then ask participants to brainstorm reasons for the "call to adventure." I like to play the devil's advocate and ask them to convince me—acting as a wary stakeholder—that this is the right route. Although they know at an intuitive level that integration offers a viable alternative, they often are unable to articulate a sound argument to support it. Some evidence is embedded in their own experiences. When asked to reflect on what and how they learned through school, few respond with comments about content; rather they remember learning the lessons of life such as "it is important to have friends," or "I learned to get my work in on time." Their reflections consist of relevant learning that was useful in real life. Within this context, educators can make sense of integrating curriculum in a world that is fundamentally changing and decide if this is an authentic path worth the struggle of traveling.

Examining Educational Beliefs

One effective entry point is to present groups with some of the endings described earlier in this chapter in the section "Letting Go of Old Beliefs." These are good triggers for dialogue and for beginning to make personal models of integration explicit.

Experience suggests that much of a person's belief system is at an implicit level; not easily accessible to pencil-and-paper measures, yet it may emerge as a major block much later in the process. To reveal the implicit, some groups have worked with developing metaphors of curriculum: popular metaphors revolve around medicine, travel, growth, ecology, and production. Horwood (1992) contrasts two different metaphors to describe different approaches to integration: the fruit cocktail and the fruit cake. In the fruit cocktail approach the chefs are teachers faced with selecting the proportion and variety of fruit to be put together to create a melange. "Fruit cocktail is a very fine dish with much capability for variation and high quality nutrition, but the component fruits retain their identity." In the fruit cake approach the disciplines persist in recognizable chunks that make sense, but they are embedded in a pervasive and unifying batter in which raw materials are unrecognizably transformed.

Questionnaire exercises may also help individuals identify their own belief systems. For example, one group used the Concerns-Based Adoption Model (CBAM) instrument (Hall and Loucks 1978) as a tool to facilitate "teacher talk." Others have successfully used the orientation inventory offered by Miller (1983) in *The Educational Spectrum: Orientations to Curriculum* (pp. 186-188).

Making Connections

Early in the process, the curriculum team should experience how easily and naturally connections across the curriculum are made. Semantic webbing, cluster and recluster, curriculum mapping, and transdisciplinary webbing are all described in some detail in Chapter 5. They are excellent exercises for groups to undertake collaboratively. Teams could work through one or all of these frameworks. Moving sequentially through the frameworks (usually with the same theme) allows people to understand the substantive differences. These exercises provide a powerful tool for talking about the connections across disciplines, rather than the differences.

The Collaborative Group Process

A newly formed curriculum team should be aware of group dynamics that occur when groups work together. Jacki Oxley, a central office team leader working with high schools, reminds her groups to expect to "form, storm, norm, and perform." That is, after a group has formed, conflict will be experienced as individuals negotiate meaning to establish a norm. Only after this can groups expect to really begin to perform. It is useful to refer to these concepts as the group inevitably begins to experience the bumps and conflicts of working collaboratively.

Teachers often work in isolation in a clearly defined hierarchal system that has not valued collaborative skills. Working together collaboratively, teams are actually learning the same skills that have been widely promoted as cooperative learning for students. Johnson and associates (1991), Clarke and associates (1990), Gibbs (1990), and Kagan (1985) offer rich descriptions of how these skills can be taught to students in the classroom. Educators learning from personal experience are in a much stronger position to facilitate students working toward true collaborative learning. As one teacher commented, "Now we have to practice what we preach."

Developing a Support Network

It is guaranteed that endings will be difficult. Rather than misunderstanding and labeling individual attitudes and behaviors as resistance, Fullan and Miles (1992) remind us to frame this period as a "natural response to transition." Supporting people and being patient as they identify the endings and experience the loss are essential.

Clearly, some introductory activities are needed to begin to build a supportive network. Some groups begin with team-building sessions. Suggested resources are *Icebreakers* (University Associates 1983) and *Silver Bullets* (Rohnke 1984). However, some team members felt these structured activities were contrived time-wasters. The team that I worked with began as six strangers interested in integrated curriculum. As team leader, I asked participants to bring their personal stories to our initial orientation meeting. Each person told how he or she had come to be selected for this curriculum venture. They also told stories of personal changes they had gone through, which we compared to the "Journey of the Hero" metaphor. Sharing their stories, team members developed an immediate sense of intimacy and respect for each other. We sensed how we were connected as humans. In hindsight, team members commented on how sharing these stories facilitated team cohesion. In later sessions, many reported, members could "risk saying anything without being censored."

Others have tried the story introduction and found it a useful way to make sincere connections. Jacki Oxley's team members were asked to share a positive educational experience and something that they contributed to education beyond the classroom. Listening to each other's stories, they discovered commonalities that became the glue holding them together. When people don't have subject expertise in common, there is a real need to find out what interests and beliefs they share.

4

The Struggle to Change

The path toward developing integrated curriculum is full of obstacles. Some of the tests and trials ahead are predictable; others are not as clear. Ambiguity, itself, is predictable; what ambiguities may be encountered is not so predictable. Some obstacles are external, others internal. One teacher, now successfully integrating, believes, "the only obstacles are the teachers themselves." For him, students have few problems with integration, only teachers do.

One optimistic team leader claims that, "we can do something about the barriers if we can name them." This section names some of the predictable obstacles that most teams can expect to encounter during the process of integration. These obstacles may be experienced either at the beginning of the process or may suddenly arise out of nowhere.

External Obstacles

School Calendar
One of the first obstacles that may be encountered is a school calendar that does not fit integrated studies. One person or department in a school often doesn't know what the next one is doing. Reviewing the school calendar is helpful here. Each teacher brings his or her curriculum to one meeting and together the staff examines existing curricular overlaps and

where natural connections can be made. Jacobs (1991) offers a useful example of calendar curriculum mapping that deals with this issue.

Advocates of integrated curriculum stress that the school calendar is only a problem if you are locked into the existing structure. They point out that the computer can be a very helpful tool in rescheduling once a school has decided to take the plunge. As one team leader put it: "You'll find out what you have to change organizationally to facilitate what you want philosophically." Another administrator summed it up by saying "Where there is a will, there is a way."

Time

Building an integrated curriculum takes a lot of time, particularly if this is the first effort. Many groups I talked to said that a period of approximately 10 days is an optimum time to build a full unit. Some extended this time over a year; others worked during summer holidays or exam periods. Often, team members would drop out or new members would suddenly be included. The groups then felt they had to move backwards. Everyone agreed that any integrated project takes "lots and lots of time." The time factor was always a shock and left people commenting that they "had no idea what we were getting into when we started."

Planning Too Much

Jacobs (Brandt 1991) suggests that the biggest obstacle to curriculum building is planning to do too much. To avoid this, she suggests beginning with natural overlaps that team members can easily identify. Full-blown units are not necessary to begin with; Tchudi (1991) recommends teachers start to introduce integrated concepts during a regular class. The people I talked to agreed with this concept. Some schools were starting with a day for the whole school or a division; others began with a week or a month program for a grade or a few classes. This fits the "jump in and do it" thinking. Graeme Barrett, a curriculum superintendent, recommends, "Start small, but think big."

When planning becomes blocked, it is time for doing. Several team leaders reported that when people tried out new ideas in the classroom, they reached new understandings, dissolved blocks, and acquired a sense of ownership. Again, this emphasizes a balance between planning and practice.

Lack of Resources

Lack of resources is a pervasive problem. Some react positively to the challenge of dealing with the problem; they point out that different members of the team can share resources rather than duplicate them. However, some districts are not rich in resources under any circumstances. The teacher librarian can be an invaluable resource. The community, too, is often an untapped reservoir.

An unexpected bonus to developing curriculum in economically tough times is that it has resulted in writing/teaching/reviewing occurring at the same time, rather than a team writing an entire unit before implementing it. One team leader observed that teachers were forced into "on the spot" reflections; curriculum emerging in these situations was particularly relevant.

Staff Turnover

Just when some teams were feeling they were gaining ground, a key member of the team, or even the principal, would move to another school. The team would then regress as members waited for a new person to work through the same steps they had already been through. One principal counteracted this by asking his staff to make a commitment to a three-year journey; those who were unwilling to do this were encouraged to seek a new school.

Leadership

The leadership of a team is problematic. Although, a team can benefit from an assigned leader, particularly in the early stages, the leader may experience difficulties if he or she is perceived to be parachuted in by the administrator. Outside leaders can also create conflicts when they are seen as subject-specific consultants protecting their own areas rather than as promoters of the team's ideas.

Having myself been in a leadership position, I was interested in the qualities that made for a good leader. I talked to a variety of people in leadership positions. Some were consultants brought in for the project; others were on the school staff and were assigned the job by the principal. Sometimes a natural leader supported by the administration emerged. I also talked to team members who had experienced different leadership styles.

Like everyone else, leaders get better with practice. The following characteristics were seen as important:
- Knowledgeable about the process
- Can see the big picture
- Allows the team to find its own voice, to do it their way
- Allows time for teacher talk, rather than "talking to"
- Can identify group patterns and articulate them
- Can synthesize the "ramblings" of a group
- Takes responsibility for the final product
- Makes people feel comfortable

- Has interpersonal skills
- Facilitates leadership evolving into collaborative shared roles.

Leaders captured the "big picture" in different ways. I kept a journal of the process as I interpreted it. I would send my team these written attempts at synthesis, which initiated discussions at our meetings and helped us to come to common understanding. Donna Carpenter, a central office member who works with K-8 schools, listened to the rambling explorations of one team and returned to the next session with a written report listing teaching strategies, learning outcomes, and assessment strategies. The group was amazed at her ability to accurately capture what they had said in a way that sounded better than they remembered saying it.

Jacki Oxley, a central office team leader working in high school settings, deliberately schedules "planned process" meetings to wrestle with differences and engage in "teacher talk." She never lets more than two writing sessions go by without such a meeting.

Isabella Peacock Snider, a central office team leader with middle school groups, emphasized that her previous knowledge of team building and group dynamics was invaluable. Other team leaders agreed, and they all expressed surprise at how much this process involved time spent counselling and building self-esteem.

The leadership of the principal is also key and may involve a graceful balancing act. Integrating teams need support and recognition. However, the rest of the staff may perceive favoritism; this can rebound as resentment toward the team and leave them feeling isolated.

Karen Erskine is a good example of a K-8 principal-leader. Karen began with a vision of a school with an integrated curriculum and holistic philosophy. She was fortunate enough to be able to hire people who agreed with her philosophy. For more than two years, an integrated team at Karen's school has been successfully planning and implementing curriculum—next year, the whole school will move in this direction. Trusting teachers' intuitions and expertise, Karen does not actively participate in curriculum planning, although she has a good working knowledge of integration. Instead, she offers a supportive environment: providing money for writing time as much as possible, arranging the school calendar to allow for teacher talk, and making a special effort to be available as a listening ear in times of trouble.

Karen's team proves that a collaborative leadership is not an impossible ideal. They began the process guided by central office consultants and supported by Karen; the original integration team members now believe that they have no defined leader and that each of them contributes equally to the process.

Evaluation

Assessment is an obstacle that many teams meet early, when it quickly becomes clear that traditional procedures won't work well. As a result, teams often leave this aspect until after they develop a unit. This may cause friction when some administrators ask, "how can you know if you've gotten there, if you don't know where you are going?" This is really an important issue—if schools cannot devise acceptable evaluation procedures that satisfy parents, the integration program will be short-lived. Alternative assessment strategies will be discussed in the next section of this booklet.

Parents/Community

Many school districts are experiencing criticism from dissatisfied parents and the community, who may view integrating curriculum as "change for change's sake." Many adults wonder why schools don't just return to the way they used to be. "After all, I turned out all right," is a common opinion. Parents need to understand the rationale for integrating curriculum as a response to a world that has fundamentally changed since their school days.

The schools that have experienced the greatest success with new programs have involved parents, the community, and local businesses. This includes open-evening meetings, newsletters, and constant communication between teachers and parents about procedural shifts. Parents may participate in program or field trips. With the new emphasis on teaching in a real-life context, teachers often take students into the community to learn from local business people. Businesses may share their expertise in school-business partnerships. Involving as many people as possible has been an excellent way to get people on board. Students, who are so often enthusiastic and involved in their integrated programs, are the strongest positive advertisement for their parents.

Reg Hawes, a curriculum coordinator for a grade 9-10 pilot project that included cross-curricular links at John Fraser School, described a formal research process to evaluate the progress of the project. The school engaged independent researchers to conduct focus group research. The focus group consisted of nine parents, nine teachers, and nine students. All participants were randomly selected. Discussions about the school program were audiotaped and transcribed. Much of the first year's research was "distressing" and indicated that changes needed to be made. However, the information gleaned from these meetings helped the school make changes that were in keeping with the school's philosophy and that also pleased people. One example is evaluation: The report cards are now eight pages long, include a proficiency scale rather than a percentage grade, and allow for anecdotal information that identifies strengths and areas for improvement. Most are happy with this new approach; at some level everyone was involved in the process.

Finally, one school district has developed a new model for evaluation where student and parental input are crucial to the process. Each student's guardian or parent is requested to attend a personal interview near the beginning of the school year to discuss and agree on desired outcomes for the student. These outcomes are based on district guidelines and parental and teacher understanding of the individual student's strengths and weaknesses. There is ongoing communication between home and school during the year as to the progress the student is making toward these outcomes. In this way there is constant feedback and the involvement of both home and school in the child's education. Although this system was not devised specifically to introduce integrated curriculum, it allows the teacher to move in this direction if this is the best path to achieving the desired student outcomes.

Internal Obstacles

The external or structural obstacles may seem formidable enough; however, it is the internal obstacles that loom as the most difficult tests ahead.

Coming to Personal Meaning

Successful educational change must take into account what each of the participants finds personally meaningful (Fullan 1991). It is lack of personal meaning that can cause the most obstinate roadblocks. Individuals who lack understanding experience anxiety and disequilibrium, and their most natural tendency is to return to old models for comfort.

Coming to personal meaning is very time consuming. Most of the groups emphasized how easy it was for teachers of different specializations to design strategies together. According to grade 9 team leader Kate Shaw, "the creative part is the easy part." Yet, no group could just develop a series of strategies and then proceed to implement them. Hours and hours of discussion, conflict, and negotiation followed strategy development. Some wrestled over the conceptual framework; others argued over the format for presenting the curriculum; a few struggled with designing appropriate activities. It didn't seem to matter what these struggles were about—they seemed to be a most necessary part of creating personal meaning.

How can curriculum teams facilitate this process of coming to personal meaning? Time. "We need lots and lots of time to talk." The curriculum writers need time for teacher talk, to sort out their questions, confusions, and sometimes ambivalent feelings.

My personal experience suggests that we need time to tell stories, to experience trial and error in the classroom, and to read existing literature on integration. Other leaders emphasize a dialectic between practice and theory. Emerging practice is often supported by theory that comes from a variety of fields. Together teams are creating new theories to guide future practice.

Anxiety/Frustration

Anxiety and frustration are predictable givens on this journey. Anxiety always accompanies the exhilaration of stepping into the unknown. "Frustrated" was a word that echoed often throughout people's stories; often people became frustrated when they felt ready to move on but others did not. It seems best to accept these emotions as guaranteed and provide support structures to help people through them. Without a supportive environment, people will inevitably return to their old belief systems and behaviors.

One strategy is to alert people to anticipate stress as normal. It is helpful to know others experience the same things. One team member, on listening to others describe their curriculum projects, remarked, "Listening to how frustrated all these other people are, I don't feel as frustrated anymore!" Team leaders Isabella Peacock Snider and Kate Shaw both experienced the stress of working on projects that devoured their time. They have learned that, "if something doesn't get done, it doesn't get done." They now set limits as to how much time they will devote to projects. Kate also talks about learning deep breathing and other stress management techniques. Time and stress management strategies can be extremely helpful to anyone involved in the process.

Vera Taylor, a principal involved in developing integrated curriculum for grade 9, believes the anxiety of being out on a limb is necessary, but she also knows that "you can be out of alignment for only so long." She tries to provide "resting points" along the path so that people can feel safe enough to continue.

Conflict

Conflict seems to be another given, and again it is helpful to know that it is normal and to be expected. As Jacki Oxley warns her high school groups, "there will be forming and storming before norming and performing." Still, there is a positive side—conflict is a catalyst for creativity. Without conflict there will be little of the creativity that is such a rewarding part of the experience.

Conflict often has a personal dimension. Kate Shaw describes it as "people struggling with their professional identity as a 'subject teacher,' conflicting with their desire to innovate." Personal conflict may also be experienced by some department heads who give up their customary role of fighting for their subject to become working members of the team. "Territorial" team members who want to ensure proper coverage of their subject areas in the curriculum set up predictable conflicts. Eventually, people come to define themselves as integrated curriculum teachers with a specialization rather than subject specialists.

Much of the conflict occurs when people meet diverse philosophies. For example, the writing of objectives or learning outcomes has caused many problems for team members who don't agree on what is important. Some members on my team insisted that the curriculum format be broken down into its smallest identifiable part; they were pitted against more global thinkers who wanted a more holistic format.

It is always difficult to resolve conflicts among team members. Several team leaders confided to me that the courses they had taken in leadership, conflict resolution, and interpersonal skills had become invaluable to them during the process. Others suggested, with rueful smiles, that the current manuals on negotiating conflict and managing difficult people were essential reading.

Because conflict is guaranteed, it makes sense to spend time learning how to reduce, negotiate, and reconcile it. Collaboration requires an "environment where intimacy and conflict coexist." It is very common for team members to take disagreements personally. Intimacy or experiencing a meaningful connection with others fosters mutual respect, which can allow team members to safely "agree to disagree." My own experiences suggest that the good of the group must prevail over the desires of the individuals. Politeness and a language of respect must rule the day. Finally, trust is a most essential ingredient that can only be built through time and experience.

This concept of "intimacy through conflict" is a helpful working philosophy. For example, when a school principal disagreed with one of the basic concepts being presented by the "expert" at an orientation session, the staff was initially horrified. The long hours of discussion that followed resulted in a clearer understanding of everyone's subjective meaning of integration. Most importantly, the team now knew that it had a safe environment in which to put dissenting views on the table.

Reg Hawes describes the school culture at John Fraser Secondary—a talented and dedicated staff committed to relevant and meaningful learning and a philosophy that "kids are first." Without integrated curriculum models to follow, the staff began by doing too much, too soon. The resulting conflict concerned not the school vision, but how to get there.

There was a silver lining to this problem: the school's "excruciatingly democratic" mode of operation meant that people felt free to "really let fly" at staff meetings. However, once they had voiced discontent they would go away and return with a creative alternative. Principal Russ Jackson is committed to a democratic culture where people—teachers, parents and students—feel that their voice can make a difference. In this milieu, people express their conflicts and use their energy to find solutions.

Dissolving the Boundaries

The more I talk to other educators integrating curriculum—from early childhood education to exit levels—and the more I read and experience, the more convinced I become that the process is essentially a dissolving of boundaries. These boundaries have been artificially imposed in an attempt to structure and order the world in a meaningful way; however, they have become accepted as reality. When people plunge into planning integrated curriculum, the boundaries are first experienced as blocks, then they crumble and dissolve. The team is then usually confronted by new boundaries and the same experience is repeated. For many teams, this dissolving of boundaries is experienced as a series of shifts or even "leaps." Just when they thought they had a new way of looking at the world, they found their newly constructed boundaries dissolving and there would be another shift or leap. This is the "uncharted territory" that so many describe. It is here that the journey is experienced as so chaotic, as two steps forward and one step back. There is no guiding light. To make the shifts, teams simply have to let go and trust the process.

Disciplinary Boundaries

The clearest examples of boundaries are the boundaries of the disciplines. For most teachers, trained as experts in a discipline, this is the way knowledge is indeed structured. Often primary or junior teachers know from their own experiences that subject areas are indeed interconnected. They express amazement at how difficult it is for a subject specialist to get around his or her version of reality. However, I have worked in districts where there was concern that even the early childhood educators were structuring curriculum according to disciplines rather than using real-life connections as the organizing principle.

Indeed, the process seems to involve a restructuring of how we perceive reality and what constitutes knowledge. In my own experience we found that interconnections were limitless. Other teams report the same experience.

Kate Shaw was "overwhelmed by the cognitive complexity . . . the links were so incredible . . . so multilayered . . . so multifaceted." Donna Carpenter reported the same experience of limitless connections when her team began to brainstorm for connections.

Different teams responded differently to this phenomena. Kate was "excited, but paralyzed, because there were so many links everywhere that it was impossible to bring them to fruition." Donna's team became overwhelmed by the limitlessness of the interconnections and retreated to safer territory by focusing the integration through "big ideas" or inquiry questions. Members of my team became fascinated by the interconnections and built this complexity into the curriculum document itself.

Although reactions were different, we all experienced the dissolving of boundaries. For many, this was a frightening experience because it meant restructuring our ways of knowing. Making sense of interconnections seems to be a universal human need. If the disciplines no longer order our ways of knowing, what will? Kate complained, "We had to have some sense of order." Her words make sense. In a world of limitless connections, humans seem to need to impose order. The disciplines accomplished exactly this: They imposed a structure to help us make sense of our world.

Learning Outcomes and Assessment Boundaries

Most teams admitted to a serious struggle when it came to addressing assessment and learning outcomes. I use the word "admitted" because there was often a sense of guilt that accompanied this struggle. Each team was well aware of the necessity of developing curriculum from a clearly established set of objectives matched by appropriate evaluation tools. Yet, when I asked them directly if they had developed these before they embarked on their teaching strategies, the answer was usually a sheepish "no."

One team had produced a document outlining very clear learning outcomes and evaluations. However, these existed because the team leader, a central office consultant, had felt strongly about their inclusion and had herself written them into the document. Another team confessed that they had no up-front "objectives" on paper although they were beginning their implementation that very week. The team leader told me she believed that each teacher in the group "intuitively sensed what the learning outcomes were." On my own team, two or three people initially insisted on learning outcomes that were differentiated into cognitive, skill, and affect. No matter how hard we tried to fit this requirement, we found it impossible to do; we proceeded with developing the document itself, leaving these questions unanswered until the end. No one seems to disagree that learning outcomes and assessment strategies should drive the process—at least theoretically. Yet, few were able to follow this in practice. Everyone was clear that the assessment procedure was critical. Yet, people intuitively sensed that evaluation in its traditional sense could not "measure" what was being taught in integrated classrooms. Uncertain how to answer the task, groups focused on "how to" do for the classroom and left the hard part until later.

This phenomenon is not meant to suggest that other teams should ignore this important area. Indeed, floundering with outcome and assessment procedures increased the sense of frustration with the writing. Yet, why was this happening when everyone knew they were going about it "the wrong way"? I believe it is because the task of developing integrated objectives and evaluation is much different than it is for traditional curriculum. As curriculum developers gain an understanding of how this can be better facilitated, the task should become easier.

Exploring the directions that people have pursued in search of learning outcomes and assessment, I heard of the same progressive shifts in dissolving boundaries. There seems to be a direct relationship between whether the connections made are identified through the lens of disciplines, skills, or a real-life context and the concreteness of the learning outcomes. The more global the connections, the more global the learning outcomes. Inextricably linked to this axiom are the assessment tools. The more the connection making veers toward acquiring real-life competencies, the more general and performance-based the assessment.

As one district moved deeper and deeper into the integration process, the learning outcomes shifted and evolved. First, they moved from identifying the knowledge, skill, and affect components to blended outcomes. This reorganization was accomplished by combing existing documents to discover the essential learnings buried within teaching activities. The vast array of subject-specific curriculum documents has been reduced to a few pages in each subject area with identified affect, skills, and knowledge components that are very general and are often blended into one statement. The traditional order has been reversed and affect is identified first; this denotes a shift in emphasis. According to Graeme Barrett, Halton district curriculum superintendent, we have had knowledge-driven programs for the last twenty years; the acknowledgement of the importance of affect has freed people to focus on a life-skills orientation.

In the next step, this summary of learning outcomes is being replaced by a one- or two-page summary of essential learnings believed to be necessary for K-12. Despite such advances, Graeme cautions, "the need for a clear understanding of what teachers are going to teach is still three to five years away . . . and potentially will always be evolving."

Districts wrestling with evaluation tend to move to more qualitative and integrated measures. In some schools, the report card is slowly changing to reflect integration. It was difficult to answer students who asked where the geography or science mark came from on their report card. The teachers were struggling to evaluate separate parts of an integrated curriculum. Today, integrated studies is being designated as a subject. Self-evaluation and instructor evaluation are being included. The teachers report that students evaluate themselves accurately, if not even a little too harshly. This is even true at the 2nd grade level. These shifts are accompanied by constant communication with parents, which leads to their understanding, acceptance, and support of the new system.

The Breakthrough Moment

In the mythological quest, the hero eventually comes to a supreme ordeal where he must slay the dragon. Campbell (1988) calls this the darkest time of all. Many of the teams I talked to described such a supreme ordeal in which, perhaps, a team breakup might seem imminent. This was true for school-based teams—one team reached a point of extreme frustration when every member wanted to quit; half of another team did quit until the rest of the people agreed to their desired compromise; members of another team conspired to "get rid of one blocking member." For Orien Calver's team, the moment came six days into a ten-day process of developing a broad-based technology curriculum. My own team came to irreconcilable differences at about the same time. One leader working with many teams identified this syndrome as happening "just past the half-way mark."

The breakthrough moment came to all these teams and could have resulted in a team breakup. Kate Shaw's perceptions of the event are worth considering. "People were getting more and more frustrated, everyone was venting about their personal frustration, myself especially. Then we experienced a breakthrough moment—a shared experience." It was after this that the team moved rapidly forward. As Kate reflects, "It was as if we all dropped our masks at the critical moment—we could see the commonalities rather than the differences."

A pattern in group dynamics is that it takes a certain number of days for a group to gel. This breakthrough may be a phenomenon of group dynamics—another reason why those who venture into this territory should be aware of the steps in the collaborative process.

Guides Through the Struggle

Following are some guidelines that can make the struggle easier.

The Wisdom of Experience

In most mythologies the hero is aided by a magical helper. For curriculum developers this magic helper is available through intuition and the wisdom gained from past experience. Teachers know a great deal about teaching from being in a classroom every day. Intuitively they know what works and what doesn't.

A reliable guide is our own experienced wisdom, which we can access if we choose to value it and listen. John Bebbington, a writer on my team, asks other curriculum writers how many collective years of teaching the members of their teams have between them. The total years of experience at the table is often amazing. Even newer teachers can claim many years of being students as past experience.

My curriculum team turned to intuition to develop a suitable evaluation unit. Based on available references, we had developed an evaluation unit that just didn't feel right. How could we authentically assess the essential learnings we believed were important? For example, we thought the ability to make connections and deal with ambiguity were important learning outcomes. How could we measure these within the context of our document? It was only when we listened to ourselves, rather than relied on other's expertise, that we reached authentic assessment.

We suggested that assessment be made on criteria such as personal engagement, ability to make connections, change management, self-direction, willingness to collaborate, and the awareness of values embedded in the learning involved in our particular approach to integration. For these criteria we offered indicators of achievement. However, we were clear that these criteria should not be prescriptive. Content and skills to be covered would be dependent on the topic being explored and the age level of the learners. We recommended that peer and self-evaluation be included in assessment strategies and that students be systematically involved in developing the criteria for evaluation.

Sharing Stories

Sharing stories is useful throughout the journey, not just at the outset. Humans organize experience and create meaning by telling and retelling stories. Consciously allowing time for and encouraging storytelling allows people to reflect on new experiences and to construct new meanings for their evolving beliefs and values. When people can't construct new meanings, they will fall back into their old habits.

As our belief systems change, so do our stories—we reinterpret events of the past. This explains how members of a successful curriculum team remember their struggles; yet, their new stories focus on the positive. Their world views have shifted. Curriculum integration becomes easier and easier.

A Supportive Environment

Throughout the change process a supportive environment from top-down to bottom-up is essential. At school, teachers need to support each other with respect for individual differences. The principal should be solidly behind the project and encourage risk-taking and learning from mistakes. Everyone involved should be aware that when educators undergo a temporary "performance dip," they are going through the essential steps to new learning. With this in mind, principals may wish to include recognition for innovation coupled with integration attempts in teacher evaluation.

Central office's support is also critical. One district chose to indicate this support by giving a school wishing to integrate curriculum a $3,000 budget to spend as they wished. They also sent in outside consultants to fill in gaps as they were needed. Today, this district has more requests than it can possibly handle and integration seems to be the direction in which the whole district is moving. In the past two years they have experienced a remarkable shift in attitudes toward integration; the enthusiasm of the high schools involved is particularly surprising and gratifying to them.

5

Three Frameworks

Two common experiences emerged among different curriculum teams. One, at a certain point the number of connections that they could make seemed limitless. Two, the boundaries of the disciplines no longer useful, each team sought a framework to organize and structure these connections in a way that made sense to them. They needed to find new, more flexible boundaries to define their world. I labeled three different ways of structuring curriculum after reflecting on my own team's experience: *multidisciplinary* focused on separate disciplines tackling the same theme; *interdisciplinary* shifted to the generic that could be found across the curriculum; and *transdisciplinary* referred to curriculum that transcended the disciplinary boundaries.

My writing team was relieved when these approaches were identified; it gave us a language to describe our experiences. The only thing that had been clear to us was that boundaries were continually being dissolved; boundaries that we hadn't even been aware of. What was not so clear as we muddled through was how each progressive leap of "boundary dissolving" emphasized a different epistemological position that affected the conceptual framework, learning outcomes, and assessment strategies. Other teams seem to have confronted the same ambiguities.

At the heart of these different approaches are serious epistemological questions. Jacobs (1989) suggests that students should study epistemological issues such as "What is knowledge?" and "How can we best access knowledge?" Curriculum developers should also address these questions. For the multidisciplinary, interdisciplinary, and transdisciplinary approaches to integration seem to have different answers. This, of course, adds to the sense of confusion and anxiety team members experience as they wade deeper into interconnections and cannot articulate the shifts in assumptions that underlie each position.

In practice, the conceptual framework for each position seems to be fundamentally different. The term conceptual framework is being used here in its simplest sense; that is, the framework from which ideas are interconnected and the rest of the curriculum development emerges. Perkins (1989) emphasizes that exploring a theme is not enough: "One needs some kind of conceptual substructure to analyze fundamental patterns and disclose important similarities and differences within and across the discipline" (p. 73). The three approaches explained in this chapter seem to drive the process of progressively dissolving the boundaries.

Finally, objectives and evaluation are an essential consideration for all curriculum design. Spady and Marshall (1991) describe a shift occurring across North America in the thinking toward objectives and evaluation. Traditionally, curriculum writers have proceeded from the Tylerian notion of systematically planning for educational experiences through written objectives identifying the behavior to be developed by the student. Spady and Marshall suggest shifting from the traditional concepts to outcome-based education (OBE) where the outcome is synonymous with the goal, purpose, and end. The traditional objectives, based on content-driven curriculum, shift to "Outcomes of Significance" based on desired changes in the learner as a starting point. OBE is based on the assumptions that all students can learn, success breeds success, and schools control the conditions of success. Many districts are moving to OBE as a way of thinking about curriculum design. However, Spady and Marshall note that there are different ways of interpreting OBE in practice. They identify Traditional OBE, Transitional OBE, and Transformational OBE as ways in which OBE is currently being practiced in the development of learning outcomes and evaluative measures. These different interpretations roughly parallel the experiences of those pursuing the multidisciplinary, interdisciplinary, and transdisciplinary approaches.

The following sections are an initial attempt at synthesizing different curriculum approaches as described by different groups navigating the process. Each approach will include an epistemological stance in the question, What is worth knowing?, a guiding conceptual framework that drives connection-making, and consideration of learning outcomes and assessment strategies. These categories are not meant to be definitive or self-fulfilling; characteristic of the process itself, the boundaries will no doubt blur or may not match the experiences of others. However, they may offer a guiding light on what often seems to be a dark and treacherous path.

The Multidisciplinary Approach

The multidisciplinary approach views the curriculum through the lens of a discipline that includes content from other disciplines to increase relevance (Figure 5.1). A discipline is easily identifiable within teaching strategies, and the discreetness of the procedures of the discipline can be kept intact by the teacher, who will probably approach the task from her own area of specialization.

FIGURE 5.1
MULTIDISCIPLINARY APPROACH

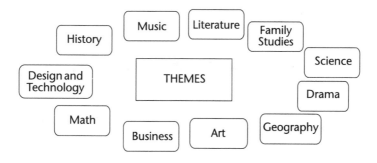

When my own team looked back, we saw that we had started by bringing our subject strengths to the table. Deciding our theme would be "car," we brainstormed for teaching strategies; they came easily and quickly. For "user friendliness," we identified each subject area in each strategy. We reasoned that subject teachers could identify their subject areas and teach within that framework.

Most teams seemed to start from a multidisciplinary framework. This was particularly true when two or three subject areas merged. Typically, when the writing process began they divided into groups or pairs with team members from similar disciplines (like math and business.) Again, the strategies flowed; however, they had a distinctly disciplinary flavor.

A multidisciplinary starting point makes sense. Teachers can still work within the context of the known. It breaks down a few of the boundaries among subject areas, but leaves the disciplines intact enough to allow teachers to continue to organize knowledge through the definition of the disciplines. Existing course content is easier to fit into an integrated model.

What is Worth Knowing?

The multidisciplinary approach asks: *what is important to learn within different disciplines?* It keeps the strength of each discipline intact; however, it encourages links between fields of knowledge so that the content has more relevance. Procedural knowledge and the skills of each discipline are presented in ways that connect them to the other disciplines.

Conceptual Framework

Semantic webbing is a simple but effective process of brainstorming connections for a theme. After selecting the theme, team members brainstorm ideas that connect to the theme (Figure 5.2).

FIGURE 5.2
SEMANTIC WEBBING

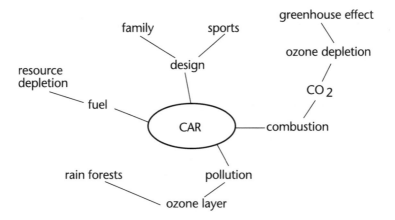

Semantic webbing is a well-known tool for primary and junior teachers. They find it extremely useful for discovering natural and obvious connections. One criticism is that the resulting curriculum may be superficial. As a conceptual framework, it can limit people to what they already know and a multidisciplinary approach. However, a semantic web can also lead teams to "too many connections" for comfort.

To increase connections, teams can also use an adaptation of the strategy of clustering and reclustering (Figure 5.3), which was developed by consultant Jan Sanders of the Institute of Cultural Affairs. For example, if team members brainstorm to create a semantic web around the theme of "car," they will then be able to cluster ideas into subthemes such as pollution, transportation, and design. After this has been accomplished, teams are challenged to recluster the data into a new set of subthemes such as war, status, and economics. This particular strategy is very effective to jolt old thinking patterns.

FIGURE 5.3
CLUSTER AND RECLUSTER

Brainstorm ideas

⟶ Cluster similar connections

⟶ Recluster new connections.

Some teams find that they are locked into the distinct disciplines (usually as a result of writing in pairs). Donna Carpenter's group found their strategies so distinctly discipline-bound that they tried a cluster-recluster solution. They recombined strategies into new subtheme clusters to create new strategies. Not yet satisfied with the degree of integration, team members recombined the new strategies once more. In this way they dissolved the boundaries and solved their problem of the curriculum not being integrated enough.

Learning Outcomes and Assessment

Learning outcomes can still be based on the procedural knowledge of the discipline. Often this is some variation of knowledge, skill, and affect. Assessment involves mastery of these procedures. Spady and Marshall (1991) point out that this is Traditional OBE, where the outcomes may not

reflect real life because they are limited to specific content details that are
driven by the curriculum.

The Interdisciplinary-Skills Approach

The interdisciplinary approach shifts from an emphasis on applying the
themes to subject areas to focusing on the commonalities across disciplines
(Figure 5.4). Given today's educational technologies and the emphasis on
metacognition, most teams turn to critical thinking skills as the organizing
principle for order and structure. Here, the content and procedures of
individual disciplines are transcended; for example, decision-making and
problem solving involve the same principles regardless of discipline. This
makes intuitive sense to teachers.

FIGURE 5.4

INTERDISCIPLINARY APPROACH

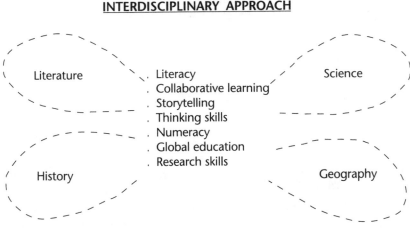

Literature

History

. Literacy
. Collaborative learning
. Storytelling
. Thinking skills
. Numeracy
. Global education
. Research skills

Science

Geography

What is Worth Knowing?

The interdisciplinary approach shifts to an emphasis on metacognition
and learning how to learn. Content lessens in importance. The question
becomes: *How can we teach a student higher order competencies?* In
integrating the subject areas, students learn that higher-order thinking skills
are generic and can be used outside the classroom.

Conceptual Framework

A curriculum planning wheel pushes the limits of semantic webbing by shifting the focus from natural connections to directing the process through the disciplines (Figure 5.5).

FIGURE 5.5
CURRICULUM PLANNING WHEEL

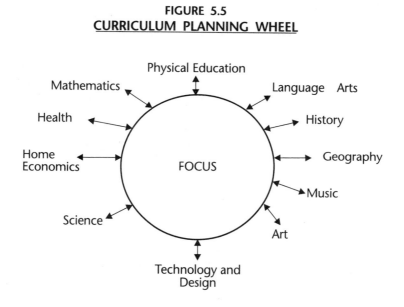

This approach is well described by Jacobs (1989) and Palmer (1991). The wheel includes as many disciplines as the curriculum writers wish and helps them make sure that no area is left out (unless the writers deem it to be a force-fit). Usually, this approach leads to a focus on generic skills across the curriculum. At this point, teams tend to work together rather than in pairs. They choose a theme and emphasize skills common to subjects. For example, the theme may be a current environmental issue such as deforestation; students apply generic research and problem-solving skills to come to a possible resolution. Jacobs (1989) suggests that a model of thinking such as Bloom's taxonomy is a good organizer that is familiar to teachers. Several subject areas might decide upon a problem or "big question" to be explored around a series of questions that follow Bloom's taxonomy and emphasize generic procedures.

Learning Outcomes and Assessment

Learning outcomes are less concrete in the interdisciplinary approach than in the multidisciplinary approach. The differentiation among cognitive, affective, and skill domains often dissolves in practice and the outcomes are expressed as "blended." (Those who attempt to do otherwise seem to find themselves in a force-fit position.) Many learning outcomes are identical across subject areas.

Assessment becomes more performance-based and beyond the boundaries of disciplines. The emphasis begins to shift to process rather than product; yet process can still be evaluated sequentially as in "benchmarks" or levels of growth that measure a student's performance. This approach roughly approximates the Transitional OBE (Spady and Marshall 1991).

The Transdisciplinary/Real-World Approach

Interconnections in the transdisciplinary approach are so vast they seem limitless; the theme, strategies, and skills seem to merge when the theme is set in its real-life context (Figure 5.6). Disciplines are transcended, but embedded naturally within the connections if one cares to look. The nature of the process of integration is such that most teams glimpsed transdisciplinary interconnections, but were often frightened at this stage and retreated to a position with more structure.

FIGURE 5.6
TRANSDISCIPLINARY APPROACH

Common Themes,
Strategies,
and Skills

What is Worth Knowing?

The question in the transdisciplinary approach shifts to: *How can we teach students to be productive citizens in the future?* This involves skills such as change management, dealing with ambiguity, perseverance, and confidence. The emphasis is on meaning and relevance through a life-centered approach; that is, knowledge is explored as it is embedded in a real-life or cultural context. The content is not considered to be intrinsically important; in fact, it is determined by the theme and student interests rather than because it has been predetermined by any guidelines.

Conceptual Framework

The transdisciplinary or real-world web emerged through the experiences of my curriculum writing team as a way of brainstorming that forced us to move beyond the dictates of the disciplines (Figure 5.7). We were working with the concept of story and wanted to understand how our knowledge was filtered through not only a "personal story" but also a "cultural story" or how knowledge was situated in a socio-political- economic context (Drake et al. 1992).

FIGURE 5.7
THE TRANSDISCIPLINARY WEB

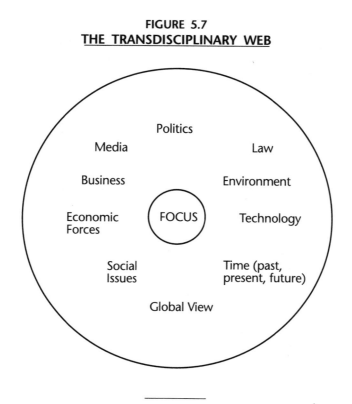

We began by using a curriculum wheel, but discovered that, to reveal the real-world context, we needed to brainstorm ideas for a theme around areas such as economics, law, media, environment, technology, politics, social issues, and time (past, present, future). When we did this the boundaries completely dissolved. When we added "global view" to the web, we were startled to discover that the theme inevitably became situated in a global context.

In working through this web with dozens of groups, I have discovered that no matter what focus or issue starts the process, the same array of vast interconnections becomes immediately apparent. Each theme is embedded in its cultural or real-life context. The transdisciplinary web does not have to use the specific categories suggested here; the trigger words should situate the object of study in its real-life context and not in one defined arbitrarily by the disciplines. One district uses systems such as communication, belief, natural, and global-social-political-economic as the trigger words.

Brady (1989) offers a vision of general education that is transdisciplinary in nature. He recommends that educators go beyond themes to a curriculum that offers a systematic model of reality that reflects the real world. He suggests that there are five major aspects of reality: environment, humans, ways of acting, ways of thinking, and how these aspects interconnect. These are everyday categories of reality that allow for the exploration of the commonplace in a framewmork that will have meaning for students. This is a spiralling curriculum where each year students tackle general education with ever-increasing levels of abstraction and complexity. For Brady, we need to teach what is essential for survival; rather than teach chemistry or history or mathematics, he wants to help students make sense of human experience. By teaching relationships educators will be asking students to use a whole range of cognitive processes; it is by engaging in these processes that human knowledge can expand.

The transdisciplinary web has been compared to using a kaleidoscope; look through one lens to see a certain pattern, shift to another lens and the same pieces exist but another pattern emerges. Another apt metaphor is a hologram—any part of the hologram holds all the pieces of the whole.

To use the transdisciplinary or real-world web, brainstorm as much information as possible around each trigger word as it applies to the chosen focus (either a topic or issue). For example, car may be chosen as the focus of the web. The brainstorming can begin anywhere. Beginning with technology and design, brainstorming might lead to the necessity to upgrade the design for safety and environmental reasons as well as to make it more marketable. This immediately connects to economics and the need to maintain jobs and produce more and more cars. The media is the strong arm that urges consumers to need and buy cars; new design is an important variable. However, cars pollute the environment, so laws must be put in place that both protect jobs and the environment—these seemingly contradictory needs result in a dilemma. And as industrialized countries continue to pollute the environment, the ozone layer is rapidly disappearing; scientists warn us that there will be a rapid increase in skin cancer; this leads to a serious social issue in health care. Enter another door of the transdisciplinary web and users discover that the same pattern unfolds.

In creating a transdisciplinary web, most groups discover that everything interconnects. This can be frightening when groups ponder how to make meaning from endless interconnections. My team decided that the best way was to focus on the connections themselves and honor this as a life skill. We also emphasized the values embedded within the web. In many ways, this exercise demonstrates that our knowledge is indeed interconnected (as opposed to fragmented) and value-laden. It can be used for values clarification. A deeper understanding of this process is offered in *Developing an Integrated Curriculum Using the Story Model* (Drake et al. 1992).

Learning Outcomes and Assessment

The transdisciplinary approach shifts our focus to core learnings that are essential, essential to living one's life in the future. Planners recognize that "the future ain't what it used to be"; that students are preparing for jobs that in many cases don't even exist yet; that the technologies they will use are not yet invented. Life skills become paramount. This includes higher-order thinking skills, but not at the expense of learning how to live in a complex world. Skills that were once considered indispensable, such as those learned in algebra, are challenged to demonstrate what they provide in helping us to live. Claire Ross, a principal of a grade 7-12 technological center developing broad based technology curriculums, suggests that the new skills should include:

- resource and information management
- applied math/science
- career planning
- technological and computer literacy
- problem solving and communication
- group interaction and human relations
- flexibility, adaptability, innovativeness
- multi-tasking.

Essential learnings are very broad and few in number, and they must be set in a context of personal relevance. Paralleling this move to broad learning outcomes is a move toward qualitative, anecdotal assessment that often requires self-evaluation as well as instructor evaluation. Parents are also involved. It is ongoing assessment that may be recorded in portfolio form. This evaluation tends to based on authentic performance rather than on examinations. Goals are reached by a variety of means. Normative expectations disappear. How can flexibility, for example, be measured on a standardized test? Instead, can students use what they have learned in a practical setting? Can they teach others? This approach closely parallels the Transformational OBE, a position promoting "higher-order, life-role performances" (Spady and Marshall 1991).

Connecting the Approaches

These approaches have been offered as a way of making meaning of curriculum integration; they are based on my own interpretation of how different groups went about making sense of integration. I do not mean to suggest that those working within multidisciplinary or interdisciplinary frameworks are not also including a real-life context and skills for the 21st century. The transdisciplinary perspective may be included within a discipline itself. Hurd's (1991) concept of an integrated science curriculum takes on a real-world or transdisciplinary flavor when he suggests it should prepare students for the 21st century and should be "a complex of interacting relationships among science, technology, society, education, and human affairs" (p. 33). In *Mathematics Assessment*, The National Council of Teachers of Mathematics (1991) promotes the view of a learner who constructs meaning and advocates using real-life problems with more than one right answer.

How do these approaches relate to one another? Through my observations, I have become convinced that the differences are more than a matter of degree, but only if educators actually pursued one approach in its purest form, as represented in Figure 5.8 on pages 46–47. In practice, these boundaries blur. The chart in Figure 5.8 is offered to help educators situate themselves philosophically and ease the trials of matching design with intention; it is not intended to set up a new set of "boxes."

My own team sensed that these were stages on a continuum that everyone would eventually go through. The stages were experienced as progressive shifts or "Aha!" leaps that occurred when a set of boundaries suddenly dissolved. The experience of others suggest that these approaches may indeed be on a continuum. Spady and Marshall (1991) state that districts seem to go through three stages of maturity in implementing outcome-based education: from focusing on existing content as a base; to developing higher-order competencies; to a broader focus of higher-order, life-role performances. For them, the shifts from Traditional to Transitional to Transformational OBE are "evolutionary."

A natural starting point for many team members has been within their own disciplines. As experts become more specialized in sub-disciplines, they can lose the sense of the whole in their field. One team working on developing a broad-based technology curriculum reported the same progressive shifts in dissolving boundaries and constructing new ways to organize the world. Their next task is to integrate with the other disciplines to develop broad-based curriculums.

A logical starting point is for two or more subject areas to get together and explore possibilities for integration. Nancy Syers, a high school English teacher, described the initial steps she made when integrating with a teacher from another subject area. After sharing philosophies, they focused on objectives or desired learning outcomes using provincial guidelines as a guide. They identified a theme they could both hook into and still honor the skills/processes, attitudes, and knowledge of their individual course of study. At this stage, the learning outcomes are tied to existing guidelines.

The next step seems to be to move into skill development. Here, teachers can creatively integrate existing curriculums and still adhere to state requirements. A teacher implementing integrated studies recalled that his team began planning with a curriculum planning wheel and developing "big questions" to direct the teaching strategies. As time went on the team shifted

1estion *What would be best for kids to learn for their
hey best learn it?* Students became more and more
culum planning. This shift occurred naturally, driven by
plementation process. Today, this teacher occasionally
whether he has included what he previously would have
areas. He seems almost surprised to realize that they
without his consciously putting them there. This is not a
. As his district has moved to integrated studies as an
this teacher no longer thinks in terms of subject-specific
concentrates on developing productive citizens of the
hift speaks to a evolutionary process.

superior to another? It seems that each one has its place,
tinuum or simply as a different way of structuring a world
nections. A transdisciplinary approach requires beginning
rather than prescription. This is an enormous leap that is
difficult, though not impossible, to reconcile with stringent state requirements. Meanwhile, the interdisciplinary position is a valid way to structure knowledge. Given recent educational technology in metacognition, this approach is probably the next step for us as we move from the known to the unknown. In Spady and Marshall's (1991) language, it seems like a

FIGURE 5.8
THREE INTEGRATED CURRICULUM MODELS

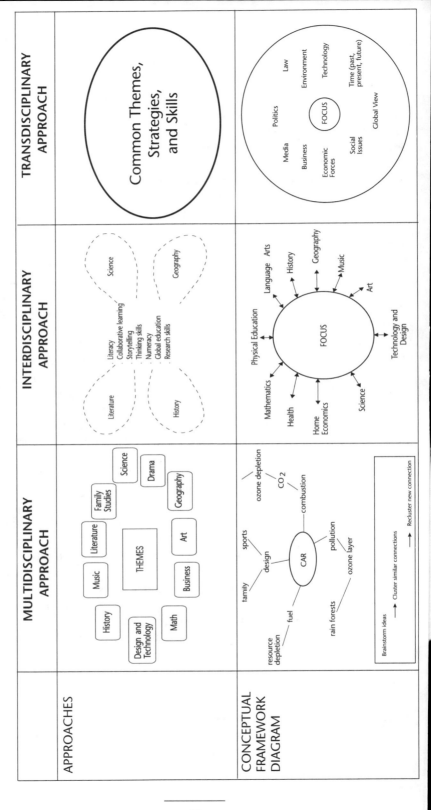

	Semantic Web / Cluster and Recluster	Curriculum Wheel	Transdisciplinary Web
CONCEPTUAL FRAMEWORK	• Semantic Web • Cluster and Recluster	Curriculum Wheel	Transdisciplinary Web
WHAT IS WORTH KNOWING?	Procedures of discipline	Procedures of generic skills (e.g., critical thinking, interpersonal)	Skills for productive citizen of the future (e.g., change management, perseverance, confidence, problem solving)
CONNECTION MAKING	Obvious connections through lens of discipline(s)	Connections across disciplines through an inquiry lens	Connections embedded in real-life context emphasizing meaning and relevance
LEARNING OUTCOMES ⇨	**discipline based** • may be cognitive, skill, and affective	**across discipline** • blended statements (cognitive, skill, and affective dimensions merge)	**essential learnings** • transcend disciplines
ASSESSMENT ⇨	Mastery of procedures of discipline	Mastery of generic skills	Attainment of life-skills (higher-order, life-role skills)

transitional position. We are still teaching prescribed skills, even though they cut across the disciplines.

For me these approaches are Chinese boxes nested in one another. For others, there will be other interpretations. Graeme Barrett, curriculum superintendent, suggests that there are many different routes to integration; the important thing is to give teams the freedom to find their own way there.

Developing Teaching Strategies

For most groups, developing teaching strategies was the easiest and most creative part of the process. However, it is helpful to have some guides to focus the activities and ensure that the teacher is teaching what he or she intends to be teaching.

Themes

Curriculum integration seems to revolve around a theme or issue that automatically breaks down the boundaries of disciplines. Several guides are available that discuss selection of age-appropriate themes and the differences among things such as concepts, topics, and categories (Fogarty 1991, Kovalik 1991, Tchudi 1991).

Projects

Projects are a popular way to integrate the curriculum. As students move through the process of completing a project, artificial boundaries dissolve. Students also come to their own meaning of integration. Horwood (1992) described a senior program combining environmental science, physical education, and English; students produced a magazine of oral history, planned and carried out wilderness trips, and performed two experiments in local research laboratories under the direction of working scientists. These students perceived integration not as overlapping disciplines or common processes and skills but as "transcendent qualities that were personally and socially significant but otherwise quite irrelevant to the disciplines" (p.6). These qualities included authenticity and involvement in a supportive community of risk takers where students felt and accepted responsibility both as individuals and as part of a group.

Problem-Based Learning

Problem-based learning organizes curriculum around real-life problems that involve a transdisciplinary context such as exploring economic, ethical, or legal considerations. Students can spend weeks or even months exploring these problems that have no easy solutions and tend to be in flux (O'Neil 1992).

Arts in Science

Many groups believe the best route to integrating curriculum is through the sciences. This ensures that the math/science component is there. Social science also seems to be a better starting point than literature. Many schools emphasize using the arts to demonstrate understanding of the learning. For example, in Lenka Tucci's 7th and 8th grade classes students were asked to develop a "creative" presentation to demonstrate what they had learned during a soil and green plants unit. Students created and performed participatory games, dramatic plays, poetry readings, storybooks, and art work. Their efforts showed an in-depth understanding of the content being explored. Such projects offer the opportunity for the "arts" to be studied in their own right. Students in this class were made aware of the art of performance and this became a part of the peer evaluation of the presentation. There were ample opportunities for other lessons in the arts to be explored. For example, one student created a wonderful children's storybook about the past, present, and future of local wetlands; she independently learned how to create pop-outs for this project and her product was the most professional. This could have offered another area for teaching in the arts.

The potential for teaching the arts in science has been well-developed by Waldorf schools. They advocate learning as a cooperative venture where the creative and artistic are emphasized. The power of imagination is most important in learning and activities are designed so that content is connected to the child's experience. For example, mathematics can be learned through story and pictures (Mollett 1991).

One possible problem with this arts in science approach is differentiating between content and strategy. For example, arts teachers may feel their area is being short-shrifted. Again, the answer lies with the power of the teachers. If a skill dimension of the arts is appropriate for the group, the skill should be taught within the context of the theme. Teaching integrated curriculum allows teachers tremendous flexibility in addressing the real needs of the students.

Student as Researcher

The student as researcher concept was very important to my project and many others see it as a crucial element. The student is perceived as a self-directed learner who can ask valuable questions and answer them through the research process. The questions that drive the curriculum then become the students' questions. The teacher librarian is a very important resource; working through a database on a computer will quickly illustrate to a student that there are no real disciplinary boundaries when exploring a theme. The other available and most important resource is the immediate world. The answers to students' questions can often be found at the local museum, at local companies and businesses, and in the stories of people within the community. Using the community as a classroom goes beyond a hands-on approach to increase the relevance of what students are learning.

Variety in Activities

To ensure variety in teaching activities, educators can use a number of available models as a checklist. Cooperative learning offers useful strategies to involve students and increase accountability. Jacobs (1989) suggests that teachers structure their questions around Bloom's taxonomy (knowledge, comprehension, application, analysis, synthesis, evaluation). Considering different ways of learning is important in planning. Lazear (1991) offers different teaching strategies that are based on the multiple intelligences defined by Howard Gardner: verbal linguistic, logical mathematical, visual spatial, body kinesthetic, musical, interpersonal, and intrapersonal. Kovalik (1991) offers a curriculum planning matrix that has Bloom's taxonomy on one axis and the multiple intelligences on the other. Teachers are urged to make sure that there is a wide enough variety in teaching activities by spreading them across the matrix.

In the classroom, teachers have found that an experiential approach is most successful. One common adage is "to make the classroom look like a kindergarten classroom." Hands-on experiences are well-received at all levels; students not only have fun while learning but are often astounded by the products they are capable of dreaming up. One high school reports good success with learning resource centers modeled after active learning centers in elementary schools. The problem with an experiential approach for some teachers is the necessity to give up time that could be used for subject skills. Asking teachers to reflect on what they remember from their own schooling often helps them to see the value of active learning.

Other models challenge educators to consider alternative ways to design teaching strategies. Clark (1986) offers an integrated learning model for learning that considers cognitive, affective, physical, and intuitive domains. Miller's (1988) concept of holistic curriculum can act as a guide that includes body/mind, logical/intuitive thinking, self/environment, and self/self connections.

Toward a Final Product

A final product seems impossible—especially in the first attempts at integration. Draft after draft can be written and rewritten and still the group is not satisfied. Part of this is tied to the process itself. The work done at the beginning does not reflect the understandings that evolve by simply going through the process. Typically, one group would generate exciting and innovative ideas for teaching activities. Then, they would spend several more days discussing the conceptual framework. But when they revisited the strategies, they would not match the framework and were not really exciting at all. My own team spent some time addressing this discrepancy between strategies and evolving beliefs; then we ran out of time and money. For us, as for many of the groups, there is still a sense of an unfinished product.

But finally, an unfinished product is really all that can be expected. Many districts now realize that the process is more important than the product. Until there is more understanding of integrated learning, there is no "right way" and there will never be enough "experts" to produce a product. The product is always evolving as the team evolves in understanding. Recognition of the unfinished quality of any written document is helpful in finding closure.

6

New Beginnings

The end of the journey marks new beginnings. The curriculum team has internalized the concept of integration and the world of education will never look the same again. This is the reward stage, a time when people experience satisfaction for a job well done. Everyone agrees the rewards are worth the struggle. The rewards include highly stimulating professional experiences that energize educators' practices. Most important, students become truly engaged and begin to talk about how much they love school. Parents are delighted by the results. Teachers continue to enjoy the challenge of working collaboratively with their colleagues.

The reward stage needs to be accompanied by a celebration, a public acknowledgment of a job well done. This may be a formal or fun event. In one district a team that has successfully planned and implemented a truly integrated curriculum is being recognized through a nomination for a district award. For another, a celebratory staff dinner marks the occasion.

7

Returning to the World

Now that the process of working collaboratively and integrating curriculum has become comfortable, the team members must return to the educational world they left behind. This is the time for service; those who know the path can share what they have learned with others.

This is already happening in Ontario. Those who have taken the journey are offering their expertise to others. I have observed several presentations where the energy and enthusiasm of the group turned a wary audience into willing participants. Concrete examples of classroom practices show the listeners there is indeed a destination to the journey.

The "experts" can shed some light upon the path ahead, although they are still discovering new and better ways of integrating. However, those who are beginning the journey must still travel the path; there seem to be no shortcuts for the trial-and-error experiences necessary for shifting ways of seeing and implementing curriculum. It will be, undoubtedly, a bumpy, messy process. Typically, as different integrated units are written they are passed on; later, the original writing team expresses surprise at how quickly a new group exhausts their ideas. In my own curriculum document we have clearly stated that the strategies suggested are only examples. We have learned that although other groups may adopt the basic concepts, they only come to subjective meaning when they develop their own strategies to fit their own situations.

8

Hearing the Next Call

We live in an age of ever-accelerating change. There certainly will be a next call to adventure. For curriculum teams this means that the first attempts at integration are forever draft documents—never good enough; never reflecting the new understandings that will evolve as the group moves through the planning and practice process. This is the nature of growth.

I had the privilege of sitting in on a planning meeting at the central office in one district. In attendance were many of the individuals with whom I had interacted to explore this process. The meeting shed some light on the next call to adventure. It was opened by a casual comment: "It's interesting how this job has no defined parameters." Everyone laughed; it clearly fit their own experiences. The conversations centered around a number of integrated projects occurring throughout the district. In describing different projects, each person referred to "the stage we're at." It has come to be a given that there are definite stages to the process and that is okay.

The district has had an overwhelming response to their offer to support new ventures in the system. Consultant Jerri Popp smiled, "We've planted the seeds and they have just grown and grown." This growth has not been without its unique problems. Now that integration has been successfully implemented in several sites, what comes next? They wanted to know how to generalize the experience to share with newcomers. People were confused by several issues—comments included "When we're talking conceptual frameworks, I don't know what we're talking about anymore," "What constitutes integrated curriculum?" "What constitutes a core learning outcome?" "When is a curriculum document ready to share with other teams?" and "Can other teams really use ready-made documents?"

Essentially, this meeting involved reflection on a movement that originated at a grassroots level; integration that began as school change has evolved to "the change" for the system. These people were struggling to see the bigger picture. Someone commented that the original projects were reactive in nature; now integration has become a proactive stance. As people explored their current experiences it became clear that the integration process is still evolving, further boundaries are dissolving, and the only guarantee is that the structures by which they have defined education are being reconstructed into new ways of thinking, believing, and behaving. They seem to be acquiring, through trial and error, the skills that will be necessary for the educators of the future to make relevant connections in a world that is ever in a state of flux and transformation. Their example may inspire others to heed the call and begin their own journeys.

References

Beane, J. (October 1991). "The Middle School: The Natural Home of the Integrated Curriculum." *Educational Leadership* 49, 2: 9-13.

Brady, M. (1989). *What's Worth Teaching? Selecting, Organizing and Integrating Knowledge*. New York: State University of New York Press.

Brandt, R. (October 1991). "On Interdisciplinary Curriculum: A Conversation with Heidi Jacobs." *Educational Leadership* 49, 2: 24-26.

Bruner, J. (1960). *The Process of Education*. Cambridge, Mass.: Harvard University Press.

Caine, R., and G. Caine. (1991). *Making Connections: Teaching and the Human Brain*. Alexandria, Va.: ASCD.

Campbell, J., with Bill Moyers. (1988). *The Power of Myth*. New York: Doubleday.

Clark, B. (1986). *Optimizing Learning*. Columbus, Ohio: Merrill Publishing.

Clarke, J., R. Wideman, and S. Eadie. (1990). *Together We Learn*. Scarborough, Ont.: Prentice-Hall Canada.

Drake, S.M., J. Bebbington, S. Laksman, P. Mackie, N. Maynes, and L. Wayne. (1992). *Developing an Integrated Curriculum Using the Story Model*. Toronto: OISE Press.

Drake, S.M. (October 1991). "The Journey of the Learner: Personal and Universal Story." *The Educational Forum* 56, 1: 47-59.

Drake, S.M. (December 1990). "The Monomyth Brings Meaning to Change." *Canadian School Executive 10:* 15-18.

Fogarty, R. (1991). *The Mindful School: How to Integrate the Curricula*. Pallantine, Ill.: Skylight Publishing Inc.

Educational Leadership. (October 1991). "Integrating the Curriculum" (theme issue) 42, 2.

Eisner, E. (June, July 1992). "A Slice of Advice." *Educational Researcher* 21, 5: 29-30.

Fullan, M. (1991). *The New Meaning of Educational Change.* Toronto: O.I.S.E. Press.

Fullan, M., and M. Miles. (June 1992). "Getting Reform Right: What Works and What Doesn't." *Phi Delta Kappan* 73, 10: 744-752.

Gibbs, J. (1990). *Tribes.* Pleasant Valley, Calif.: Center for Human Development.

Hall, G., and S. Loucks. (1978). "Teacher Concerns as a Basis for Facilitating and Personalizing Staff Development." *Teachers College Record* 80, 1: 36-53.

Hargreaves, A., and L. Earl. (1990). *Rights of Passage.* Toronto: Ontario Ministry of Education.

Horwood, B. (June 1992). "Integration and Experience in the Secondary Curriculum." Paper presented at the Canadian Society for Studies in Education Charlottetown, Prince Edward Island.

Hurd, P. (October 1991). "Why We Must Transform Science Education." *Educational Leadership* 49, 2: 33-35.

Jacobs, H.H. (October 1991). "Planning for Curriculum Integration." *Educational Leadership* 49, 2: 27-28.

Jacobs, H.H., ed. (1989). *Interdisciplinary Curriculum: Design and Implementation.* Alexandria, Va.: ASCD.

Johnson, D., R. Johnson, and E. Holubec. (1991). *Cooperation in the Classroom,* revised edition. Minn.: Interaction Book Company.

Kagan, S. (1985). *Cooperative Learning Resources for Teachers.* Riverside, Calif.: University of California.

Kovalik, S. (1991). *Teachers Make the Difference—With Integrated Thematic Instruction.* Village of Oak Creek, Ariz.: Books for Educators.

Lazear, D. (1991). *Seven Ways of Knowing: Teaching for the Multiple Intelligences.* Pallantine, Ill.: Skylight.

Miller, J. (1983). *The Educational Spectrum: Orientations to Curriculum.* New York: Longman.

Miller, J. (1988). *The Holistic Curriculum.* Toronto: O.I.S.E. Press.

Miller, J., B. Cassie, and S. Drake. (1990). *Holistic Learning: A Teacher's Guide to Integrated Studies.* Toronto: O.I.S.E. Press.

Mollett, D. (October 1991). "How the Waldorf Approach Changed a Difficult Class." *Educational Leadership* 49, 2: 55-56.

National Council of Teachers of Mathematics. (1991). *Mathematics Assessment.* Reston, Va.: The National Council of Teachers of Mathematics.

O'Neil, J. (August 1992). "Rx for Better Thinkers: Problem-Based Learning." *ASCD Update* 34, 1: 3-4.

Palmer, J. (October 1991). "Planning Wheels Turn Curriculum Around." *Educational Leadership* 49, 2: 57-60.

Perkins, D.N. (1989). "Selecting Fertile Themes for Integrated Learning." In *Interdisciplinary Curriculum: Design and Implementation,* edited by H. H. Jacobs. Alexandria, Va.: ASCD.

Rohnke, K. (1984). *Silver Bullets: A Guide to Initiative Problems, Adventure Games, and Trust Activities.* Dubuque, Iowa: Kendall-Hunt.

Spady, W., and K. Marshall. (October 1991). "Beyond Traditional Outcome-Based Education." *Educational Leadership* 49, 2: 67-72.

Tchudi, S. (1991). *Travels Across the Curriculum: Models for Interdisciplinary Learning.* Richmond Hill, Ont.: Scholastic.

University Associates. *Icebreakers.* (1983). San Diego: University Associates.